To

_____

From

_____

Date

_____

God Moments
for
GIRLS

✝

CHRISTIAN ART
PUBLISHERS

Published by Christian Art Publishers
PO Box 1599, Vereeniging, 1930, RSA

© 2019
First edition 2019

Devotions adapted from *One-Minute Devotions for Young Women*
by Mallory Larsen

Cover designed by Christian Art Publishers

Images used under license from Shutterstock.com

Scripture quotations are taken from the *Holy Bible*, New Living
Translation, copyright © 1996, 2004, 2015 by Tyndale House
Foundation. Used by permission of Tyndale House Publishers,
Inc., Carol Stream, Illinois 60188. All rights reserved.

Scripture quotations are taken from the *Holy Bible*, New
International Version® NIV®. Copyright © 1973, 1978, 1984, 2011
by International Bible Society. Used by permission of Biblica,
Inc.® All rights reserved worldwide.

Scripture quotations are taken from the *Holy Bible*,
Contemporary English Version®. Copyright © 1995 by American
Bible Society. All rights reserved.

Scripture quotations are taken from the New Century Version®.
Copyright © 2005 by Thomas Nelson, Inc. Used by permission.
All rights reserved.

Scripture quotations are taken from the *Holy Bible*, English
Standard Version®. Copyright © 2001 by Crossway Bibles,
a publishing ministry of Good News Publishers.
Used by permission. All rights reserved.

Scripture quotations are taken from The Message. Copyright ©
by Eugene H. Peterson, 1993, 1994, 1995, 1996, 2000, 2001, 2002.
Used by permission of NavPress Publishing Group.

Set in 10 on 13 pt Ulio by Christian Art Publishers

Printed in China

ISBN 978-1-4321-3082-4

19 20 21 22 23 24 25 26 27 28 – 10 9 8 7 6 5 4 3 2 1

Introduction

Use these special God moments to make every moment of the day a joy-filled adventure.

You don't need to face every day on your own, you have God by your side. By reminding yourself of His presence, you will be able to celebrate every moment of every day, knowing that anything is possible with Him.

Start your day off right by spending time with God. Gift yourself a moment with Him as you read through the short devotion and key Bible verse. See your faith grow as you have a God moment every day!

Fitting in

"Do not be afraid, for I have
ransomed you. I have called you
by name; you are Mine."

ISAIAH 43:1

Do you ever feel like you just don't belong? Does it feel like everyone has a place where they fit in except you? It's difficult to see a tight-knit group of friends together while you are left feeling alone and unseen.

It feels good to have a place where you fit in and, thanks to God, you do!

You are God's beloved creation. He calls you by name and sees how unique you are. Know that you will always have a place as a daughter of the King.

Uniquely gifted

In His grace, God has given us different gifts for doing certain things well.

ROMANS 12:6

I wish I could sing. She's so funny. I'm always so clumsy. Does this sound like you? When you focus only on the skills you lack or the things other people can do better than you, you are putting yourself down for no good reason.

Our Creator God is not boring. What sort of world would it be if we each had the same gifts? Billions of talented singers, athletes, scientists or comedians would make for a pretty boring world.

What are you good at? Embrace your God-given talents and thank God for them.

Celebrate joy

The joy of the LORD is your strength!
NEHEMIAH 8:10

Who doesn't love a good party? It is fun to celebrate birthdays, graduations and other big events with friends.

If celebrating is so much fun, though, why wait for a special occasion? Can't the goodness we experience with good food and laughter be enough of a reason to get together?

Knowing and living a life with God gives us a deep joy that can hardly keep us from wanting to throw a party!

So, why not? Invite friends and people you may not know very well. Let everyone enjoy food, drink, laughter, conversation and the gladness of God's presence.

Team building

Encourage each other and build each other up.

1 THESSALONIANS 5:11

Imagine playing on a competitive sport team that wants each teammate's best performance. What happens when one player messes up?

While it can be frustrating when a team member makes a mistake, it seems quite senseless to punish them for it.

As human beings, it is impossible to have a team that is made up of perfect members. We will all mess up in one way or another. Instead of belittling one another, let's build one another up when we fail, rather than tear each other down even more.

Happy ever after!

God will wipe away every tear from their eyes. There shall be no more pain.

REVELATION 21:4

Think about all of the movies that have "fairytale endings." The big problem is solved, the girl and guy get together and everyone lives happily ever after.

What happens, though, when we turn the movie off and get back to real life? Where is our happily ever after then?

Well, here's the good news: Living for God means that we are guaranteed the ultimate "happily ever after!" Our eternity in heaven will be filled with joy, better than any movie ending we can even imagine!

Set an example

Don't let anyone think less of you because you are young. Be an example to all believers.

1 TIMOTHY 4:12

Who do you look up to? Whose example are you following?

Do you only look up to those who are older, or do you take note of the words and actions of your friends, too?

It can be easy to assume that no one will look up to us until we are older. It's true that we can learn a lot from older people, but we are never too young to set an example of what it means to live a godly life.

Be a good example to those around you!

A true knight

Say to those with fearful hearts, "Be strong, do not fear; your God will come."

ISAIAH 35:4

Do you ever just want to be rescued? It doesn't have to be a knight in shining armor riding in on a white horse, but someone to take away our troubles would be nice!

What we have is better than a knight on a white horse. God is our rescuer, committed to saving us from the things that harm, terrify or worry us.

God is here for today's troubles and He is already on the way to fight off tomorrow's troubles.

One step at a time

**Faith shows the reality of what
we hope for; it is the evidence
of things we cannot see.**

HEBREWS 11:1

You're walking down the staircase in your home at night, without any lights on. You know that there are stairs leading all the way down, but you are afraid that you'll miss one, slip and fall.

Similarly, holding on to our faith in God can be scary. Having faith in Him means that we keep taking the next step, even if we cannot see where it is.

In this life, we might miss a step, trip and fall, but we can trust that God is with us, guiding us to the next step.

Making a mistake

The kind of sorrow God wants us to experience leads us away from sin and results in salvation.

2 CORINTHIANS 7:10

Sometimes, when we make a mistake, an adult may ask us what we learned from our misstep. While we may feel like this is just part of being punished, it's actually a question God wants us to be asking throughout our lives.

Sin is not only something we should say sorry for, it is something that can teach us and help us to walk closer to God. This means that our walk with God can be strengthened, even when we do something wrong!

Learn from your mistakes and you will already be closer to God.

Praise the Lord

Shout to the LORD, all the earth; break out in praise and sing for joy!

PSALM 98:4

Do you ever sing while you're in the shower? What about cheering at a sporting event?

We human beings were created to make noise! And you know what? God loves to hear the sounds we create—especially when we make a noise praising Him.

We really don't need to be at church, with an instrument or in a group to worship God. We can yell. Clap our hands. Snap our fingers. Play the drums on our kitchen counter.

Praise His holy name loudly, proudly and creatively, wherever you can!

Faith in training

Consider it pure joy whenever you face trials, because you know that the testing of your faith produces perseverance.

JAMES 1:2-3

We can't simply wake up one morning and run a marathon. We have to train for it and there will be days when we have to face setbacks.

This is when we have to persevere.

It is not much different in our faith journey. We will sometimes feel like we have to do the impossible, but each experience, be it a setback or a win, is helping us to get ready for the next part of our journey of faith! So don't give up.

Show & tell

> "Your love for one another will prove
> to the world that you are My disciples."
>
> JOHN 13:35

In what ways do you tell people that you believe in God? Do you tell them that you are a Christian? Carry your Bible with you?

This is all good, but "showing" can often be more powerful than "telling."

When we bring food to the hungry, water to the thirsty, or a hug to the lonely, we are not only telling them, through our actions, that we are a child of Christ, we are showing them what it looks like to be a follower of Jesus. We are making a difference in their lives.

Be positive

A cheerful heart is good medicine.

PROVERBS 17:22

If complaining was difficult, do you think anyone would actually do it? It's incredibly easy to complain about things!

For many of us, complaining takes no effort, while speaking positive or encouraging words sometimes requires us to dig a little deeper into how we see a situation.

The thing about complaining, however, is that it can so easily suck the joy out of our lives! Nobody likes to be around a constantly negative person.

Being negative all the time makes it nearly impossible to see the good in any situation and hard to see God in it too.

As we speak positive words, we can encourage others — and ourselves!

Where is God?

Since the world was created, people have seen the earth and sky. Through everything God made, they can clearly see His invisible qualities.

ROMANS 1:20

Where do you notice God? Do you become aware of His presence while in church? Maybe you see God's presence while walking in nature.

The amazing part is that all we need to do is open our eyes and look around — God is everywhere! He created the trees, the flowers, the animals and the mountains. He made the faces we pass on the street and the sun that shines on our faces.

When we are struggling to find God, let's take a moment to notice the things around us. He created it!

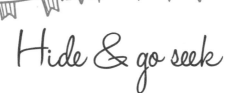

Hide & go seek

"You will seek Me and find Me when
you seek Me with all your heart."

JEREMIAH 29:13

Have you ever played a game of Hide & Go Seek? Nothing beats finding the ultimate hiding spot, making it nearly impossible for anybody to find you.

Can you imagine if life with God was like a game of Hide & Go Seek? Sometimes it feels that way.

We look high and low, far and wide, wanting to feel close to Him. To God, though, our relationship with Him is no game. He doesn't look for the most unthinkable hiding spot and then wait as we run past Him countless times. Instead, He tells us that He has no good hiding spot. When we seek Him, we will find Him.

Telling the truth

I confessed all my sins to You
and stopped trying to hide my guilt.
And You forgave me!

PSALM 32:5

Keeping a secret from someone is hard work, especially when the secret involves something you did wrong.

Sure, it might seem easier to keep it from them than to confess what you've done, but the guilt of keeping that secret can wear you out.

What if, on the other side of telling the truth, there is freedom — full freedom from feeling guilty and ashamed?

Maybe you're withholding something from a friend or family member, or maybe even from God. Remember that we have the promise of God's forgiveness. So don't be afraid to tell the truth.

More like Jesus

The Lord – who is the Spirit – makes us more and more like Him as we are changed into His glorious image.

2 CORINTHIANS 3:18

Do you and your friends dress alike? It is not uncommon for us to look, dress or act in the same way as those we live around and spend time with.

The more time we spend with God, the more we will change into His image. We might begin trying to speak like Him or act like Him, leading to us looking more like Him!

It's fun to share clothing and music with our friends, but how much better would it not be to become more like Jesus!

Teamwork

"My grace is all you need. My power works best in weakness."

2 CORINTHIANS 12:9

Teamwork is a wonderful thing. We were meant to do life with others, to help and be helped.

At what point, however, in our own personal journeys do we find ourselves needing to stop and ask for help?

Once we can admit that we have reached our limit, it becomes easier to ask for help.

If we know that we, all alone, cannot do something, we can invite both God and others to help us. When we can say that a task needs to be done by "we," and not "I," then the task is already easier — before it has even begun!

Love of beauty

Your heart was filled with pride because of all your beauty. Your wisdom was corrupted by your love of splendor.

EZEKIEL 28:17

How many times a day do you find yourself looking in a mirror? Do you take and retake "selfies" until you have the perfect shot? How much time do you spend thinking about your appearance?

It is good to feel confident and beautiful, but when it becomes more important than other things, we know that we're chasing after pride.

Today, may you love what you see when you look in the mirror, but may you focus more deeply on what cannot be seen in that reflection — your relationship with God!

Zoning out

We must pay the most careful attention, therefore, to what we have heard, so that we do not drift away.

HEBREWS 2:1

You're in school or at summer camp — all places where instructions, warnings and helpful tips are offered regularly.

Do you ever find yourself simply zoning out? Maybe you're tired or have too many other things on your mind; maybe you think you have all of the information you need, so listening to further instruction seems pointless.

When we're always zoning out, we could miss some genuinely helpful information. The same is also true for the instructions we receive in the Bible — no matter how often we've heard it, let's listen again, keeping God's instructions close to our hearts!

A hiding place

You are my hiding place;
You protect me from trouble.

PSALM 32:7

Do you have a go-to spot when you feel scared or lonely? Maybe you climb under your bed, crouch in the bathtub or have a favorite tree you like to climb. It is nice to have a place we can escape to when we don't feel all that great. But what if you cannot go to your favorite spot?

Anywhere we are, at home or at school, we can find a safe spot in God.

We don't need to be in a particular spot (though it is sometimes nice to have our own special spot!), but we can stop where we are and pray.

Free time

A hard worker has plenty of food, but a person who chases fantasies has no sense.

PROVERBS 12:11

How do you spend your free time? Do you know the hours in a day that you spend on social media, or watching TV?

When activities that give us a chance to rest become a focus of the day, eating up minutes that could be spent doing more important things, then the things that make us unique in the world starts to fade. Our potential fades, even if only slightly.

Give yourself the rest you need while continuing to do what it is you were put on this earth to do — shining God's light for others.

Saying sorry

"Even if that person wrongs you seven
times a day and each time turns again
and asks forgiveness, you must forgive."

LUKE 17:4

I'm sorry" is a phrase that is meant to hold a great deal of meaning, but it is so easy for most of us to spout it out to others out of habit rather than a genuine apology. How do you respond when an "I'm sorry" is quickly tossed in your direction with, seemingly, little meaning?

While it doesn't feel good to receive half-hearted apologies, we can continue to offer the same forgiveness that God offers us. You can lovingly forgive others and trust that God will work in their hearts.

Feeling rejected

"Those the Father has given Me will come
to Me, and I will never reject them."

JOHN 6:37

At some point in our lives, we all face some sort of rejection — and it is miserable.

Few things make us feel more lonely and depressed than being told that we are, essentially, not good enough.

We can know for sure though that God will never reject us. Our relationship with Him is a safe relationship.

So if you are feeling like an outcast and lonely, take comfort in the relationship you have with God. He will never reject you.

Friends for life

As iron sharpens iron, so a friend sharpens a friend.

PROVERBS 27:17

What are some of your favorite things to do with your friends? Do you go shopping, see movies or listen to music?

It is a great blessing in life to have friends with whom we can have fun, laughter-filled, light-hearted experiences. What a gift!

When we trust and respect our friends, we have people we can depend on. Our friendships should be a place where we can freely admit to making mistakes, receive forgiveness and be corrected in love.

We should definitely be enjoying our time with friends, but we should also allow those relationships to grow.

Excited about God

I am not ashamed of the gospel, because
it is the power of God that brings
salvation to everyone who believes.

ROMANS 1:16

Have you ever been so excited about something that you could hardly contain your enthusiasm? Maybe you were offered a spot on a sports team, or won a prize at the county fair.

When we accept God's love and presence in our lives, the reality of it is so great that we might actually be bursting to share it! It makes God so happy to see that, and He wants us to share it with others.

We have been saved and get an eternity with Jesus in heaven — that definitely sounds like something to shout about!

God loves you

May you have the power to understand how wide, how long, how high, and how deep His love is.

EPHESIANS 3:18

Do you know how deep the ocean is, how high the sky is or how many stars speckle our universe?

There are things in this world that our minds simply cannot fully understand. Of all of those things, however, God's love for us should be among the most powerful.

How many different animals or colors exist in creation? We might think we know, but we cannot be certain!

Can you say how wide, long, high and deep God loves you? Because I bet it's a bit wider than that — and a bit longer, higher and deeper, too.

Being proud

"Those who exalt themselves will be humbled, and those who humble themselves will be exalted."

LUKE 14:11

Don't you love leaving the house wearing a brand-new outfit?

Maybe you're rocking a great pair of sneakers and perfect-fitting jeans. As the day goes on, you might become more and more aware of how many people are staring at you. What a great feeling!

Before you know it, you may not even care what people think about your personality anymore, as long as they think you're beautiful.

This is pride and God hates pride. There is nothing wrong with thinking of yourself as beautiful, but be careful that the way you look does not become the most important thing in your life.

Never gossip

"Do not judge others, and you will not be judged."

MATTHEW 7:1

When you're with a friend who continually gossips about and judges others, do you ever find yourself wondering if she is saying similar things about you when you're not around? What a horrible feeling!

What do others think about us based on what we say? Maybe we try to save our harshest comments about people for the ears of our closest friends. But, no matter who is listening, what we say still says something about us. When we judge others, we are opening ourselves up to being judged ourselves, not only by the people around us, but also by God.

Only speak what is true and encouraging to others.

Patiently wait

Wait patiently for the LORD.

PSALM 27:14

When someone is a few minutes late to pick us up or our food at the restaurant takes longer than we'd like, we can get a little antsy!

We live in a world where we can get most things in an instant. Text messages can be received without delay, and easy access to the Internet allows news to spread across the globe in a matter of minutes. It's no wonder, then, that we are not so good at waiting!

We need to learn how to be patient. It will not be easy! Some good things come quickly, but many others come to those who know how to wait for them. Waiting builds good character and trust in God!

You're invited

"There is more than enough room in My Father's home."

JOHN 14:2

Have you ever attended a "first come, first served" event? A show at school, perhaps, that only has a limited number of seats. In order to see the show, you have to arrive several hours before the time, or have a friend save you a seat.

In the kingdom of God, we don't need to worry about beating the lines or pushing others out of the way in order to get a spot. We don't even need our friends to save us a seat, because God has already assigned us our own seats. You are guaranteed a place at God's table, and there is room to invite others as well!

Me, myself and I

You are boasting about your own
pretentious plans, and all
such boasting is evil.

JAMES 4:16

Look at my new cell phone! Guess what happened to me at school today! I am so busy these days! That fantastic new bag is all mine!

Have you ever noticed how many things you say that are all about you? It can be pretty easy to talk about ourselves; after all, we're with us every day! But the more we talk about us, the less we're asking about others. This is not what God wants. He asks us to love others well.

Share your life with others, but don't forget to make space for "you," "your" and "ours," not just "me."

Being joyful

I will continue with all of you for your progress and joy in the faith.

PHILIPPIANS 1:25

Do you remember when you first learned to swim? Getting into the water without knowing how to stay afloat can be a pretty scary experience! However, swimming is an important skill to have, and so we are encouraged to "stick with it!" Eventually, our commitment pays off and swimming even becomes fun!

As we stay committed to God, we will grow more comfortable and joyful! There may still be difficult times but we will be able to get through them with God's help.

The more we commit to God, the more joyful we will become!

Stain remover

**Create in me a pure heart, O God,
and renew a steadfast spirit within me.**

PSALM 51:10

Grease stains are the enemy of nearly anyone who has spent some time in a kitchen! These stains are known for their staying power! What's important to note, however, is that,.generally, they are possible to remove. It takes a great deal of patience, willpower, and the correct stain remover, but grease stains can come out of the clothing they soak into!

When we think about our poor decisions and missteps, it's easy to be discouraged by our "badness." We can start to feel too far gone, as if our heart and soul are all covered in grease stains. But no sin is beyond God's forgiveness; He can take care of it!

Following the rules

**We can be sure that we know Him
if we obey His commandments.**

1 JOHN 2:3

You may have specific rules you need to abide by on your sports team, a dress code at school, or a curfew at home.

Whatever the rules are, you know that in order to belong and not get kicked out, you must abide by those rules.

Belonging to Christ is an invitation that is available to everyone! However, God has shared commandments with us that we have to follow. So just as we know we belong to a certain sports team when we wear their uniform, we can feel confident in our place in God's kingdom as we obey His commandments.

Loving others

**love never gives up, never loses
faith, is always hopeful, and endures
through every circumstance.**

1 CORINTHIANS 13:7

Dogs are always excited to see us, rarely
hold a grudge and stay focused on what
they want. They comfort us when we're sad,
play with us when we're joyful and serve
as our best friend, no matter what happens.
We can learn a lot about love from our dogs.

When we're struggling with how to love
someone, let's think about what our most
loving and loyal dog would do.

We need to support our family and friends,
even when life gets tough, and we should
always believe the best about them.

On God's mind

The LORD is close to all who call on Him.

PSALM 145:18

Have you ever called a friend who answered the phone by saying, "I was JUST thinking about you!" How cool is that!? We feel a deep connection with someone anytime we find out that we were thinking about one another at the same time.

This is how it is with God when you call to Him in prayer. His initial response to you will consistently be just the same, no matter how or why you're contacting Him: "Hi!" He'd say, "I was JUST thinking about you!"

No matter how long it has been since you've called to God, He will have already been thinking about you.

One Creator

God who takes care of me will
supply all your needs from
His glorious riches, which have
been given to us in Christ Jesus.

PHILIPPIANS 4:19

When you see someone familiar, do you ever think about how you are warmed by the same sun and sit under the same sky? It's fun to think about the things we share with other people!

The same God created us, our neighbors, the strangers in the grocery store and the men and women who walked the earth alongside Jesus Christ. Things like culture, hobbies and sports may unite small groups of people, but God's love for us and His promises to us unite all believers everywhere!

Hearing God

"The gatekeeper opens the gate for him, and the sheep listen to his voice. He calls his own sheep by name and leads them out."

JOHN 10:3

You're walking down the road when you hear a familiar voice. Without even having to see her face, you know that it is your friend. You can make out your friend's voice before even seeing her because you know her; her voice is familiar to you.

Are we familiar enough with God's voice that we could recognize Him as easily as we do our friend?

The more we talk (and listen) to God, the better we will get to know His voice; when we know His voice, we'll know when it is Him guiding us!

A happy ending

"In Me you may have peace. In this world you will have trouble. But take heart! I have overcome the world."

JOHN 16:33

Although we may know the ending of a movie, it is still fun to watch! Just because everything eventually works out does not mean that the story will be without action, surprises and heartache.

The same is true for our time on earth. We know the end of the story! We know that Christ will come back and that He will take us with Him to heaven! However, that does not mean that we won't face difficulties.

The best part about knowing the ending is that we can hold on to hope, even when the middle gets painful.

Giving gifts

"Give, and you will receive."

LUKE 6:38

You give a friend a present for her birthday; your friend gives you a present for yours! It might be the polite thing to do or it may be what we are expected to do. Either way, when we give something, then we get something.

God says that if we give to others, whether we are friends with them or not and whether we get something from them in return or not, then we will be blessed.

When we give gifts, our generosity will return to us, though it may not come from those we give to — God will meet our generosity with blessing!

God loves you

**Give thanks to the LORD, for He is good!
His faithful love endures forever.**

1 CHRONICLES 16:34

Loving others means tolerating many not so nice things. We hurt and disappoint one another more often than we would like to admit.

Do you know the limits of what your love can take? Is it when you are lied to, cheated on or stabbed in the back?

We are less than perfect people in a relationship with a perfect God, which makes us guilty of hurting and disappointing Him, too.

His love for us can take anything. No level of anger, backstabbing or disrespect will change it. This does not give us permission to treat God badly, but if we do, His love for us will remain.

Following God

Are there those among you who
are truly wise and understanding?
Then they should show it by living
right and doing good things with a
gentleness that comes from wisdom.

JAMES 3:13

Imagine that you have a choice between two roads. One is filled with sharp turns, deep potholes and unexpected obstacles. It is dangerous, uncomfortable and scary. The other road, however, is smooth, well paved and relatively straightforward. Which one would you choose?

If we live our lives following God, we will be building a steady foundation. Our relationship with God will offer us a more stable road for the journey. That does not mean it will always be easy, but we will have God's love, protection and promises to help us.

Alone at night

Even when I walk through the darkest valley, I will not be afraid, for You are close beside me. Your rod and Your staff protect and comfort me.

PSALM 23:4

What is scarier than walking in the dark? Walking in the dark alone. By ourselves, we feel more at risk and can easily imagine hearing scary noises. When we're with someone else, we feel the power in numbers — having someone with us helps to keep our fears and imagination at bay.

When you are walking in the dark or find yourself in a difficult situation, you can find strength in remembering that you are never alone! God walks with you to both protect and comfort.

Know that the power of His presence will protect you.

Being a good friend

A friend is always loyal, and a brother is born to help in time of need.

PROVERBS 17:17

Sometimes being a good friend simply means answering the phone. It is saying, "Yes," even when you'd rather say no. We may not be able to "fix" all of our friends' troubles, but we can be there for them.

Being a good friend is being there for someone. That could mean checking up on them when they're ill, going to their sports event, encouraging them to never give up on their dreams, or praying for them on a regular basis.

Life is tough; we need each other. Let's not underestimate the power of showing up!

Surprise yourself

All glory to God, who is able,
through His mighty power at work
within us, to accomplish infinitely
more than we might ask or think.

EPHESIANS 3:20

Have you done something you never had the guts to do before? Perhaps you sang a solo at the school concert, or tried out for the hockey team? It's so fun when we are able to surprise ourselves with our own courage and abilities.

God also loves to surprise us, not only with the wonderful things He can do in our world, but also with the things He does through us.

What is He doing in and through you these days? Let yourself be amazed!

You are forgiven

Let us come near to God with a
sincere heart and a sure faith,
because we have been made free from
a guilty conscience, and our bodies
have been washed with pure water.

HEBREWS 10:22

When you hurt someone, the guilt you feel can make it difficult to face them, even after they have forgiven you. Trust that when they forgive you they truly mean it. You can face them knowing that your relationship will continue on.

The same is true in our relationship with God. We can trust that His forgiveness is real. Whatever guilt we've been carrying with us can be set aside; we've been forgiven, and our relationship with Him carries on!

Fighting back

**Never pay back evil with more evil.
Do things in such a way that everyone
can see you are honorable.**

ROMANS 12:17

Have you ever seen students taunt each other? It does not take long before both are angry. But what if one girl decided to keep the peace by not taking part in teasing the other? How quickly the situation would change!

In what ways do we return the taunts of others in order to defend ourselves? It is hardly possible to imagine a world where no one would seek revenge; but we can do our part to block the return of unkind words and actions.

Being a bearer of peace means we should not get angry and say mean things in return!

Words matter

"The words you have said will
be used to judge you. Some of your
words will prove you right, but some
of your words will prove you guilty."

MATTHEW 12:37

Do you ever read the hurtful comments on social media? Or have you sent a mean message to a friend? Our words can get pretty ugly. But the words we use reflect who we are.

Whether we're sending a text message, sharing our thoughts on social media or talking to someone face-to-face, what we have to say actually says a lot about the condition of our own hearts.

Before you speak, ask yourself if your words are honoring God. If they're not, talk to God about what you're feeling.

Don't worry

**The LORD gives perfect peace
to those whose faith is firm.**

ISAIAH 26:3

There are no shortages of things to stress about these days. The pressures of having good grades, do well in sport, be cool and have a group of awesome friends are enough to keep most girls up at night. But it does not have to be this way!

God wants to be closer to you than your own worries. The peace of God is greater than the stresses of the world, and that peace can cover you whenever you focus on Him.

Whatever your circumstances, God longs to step in and silence your anxiety with perfect peace.

Trust God

Don't love money; be satisfied with what you have. For God has said, "I will never fail you. I will never abandon you."

HEBREWS 13:5

Think of all the things you rely on each day, often without giving it a second thought (until they don't work). The lights in your home, your phone, and your body's senses are a few examples. While many of these often work for years at a time, everything manmade will one day stop working.

If we so naturally rely on things that we know will one day fail us, what is stopping us from wholly relying on God, who will never fail us?

Many of today's technologies are incredible tools to aid in our everyday lives. However, they are not replacements for God's presence. In fact, nothing is.

The name of Jesus

At the name of Jesus everyone will bow down. And to the glory of God the Father everyone will openly agree, "Jesus Christ is Lord!"

PHILIPPIANS 2:10-11

"Encore, encore!" At the end of a performance, this word is shouted to try and get the band to play another song. With that word, musicians know they are being summoned back on stage; it is a form of flattery, a call to action.

One day, the name of Jesus will be a call to action that is honored by all. When it is spoken, we will bow down in worship, amazed by the peace that even the sound of His name can bring.

One day, we will all hear His name as a call to pause, to worship and to love — and we will all understand.

You belong

The human body has many parts, but the many parts make up one whole body. So it is with the body of Christ. We have all been baptized into one body by one Spirit.

1 CORINTHIANS 12:12-13

It feels really good to feel like we belong in a group of people. It's nice to feel missed when we're not there. There is something that makes us all long to be needed. Maybe you are not currently part of a team. Even still, no matter where you are, you belong to a larger community.

We are children of God. We have a place here; our presence is needed here.

We need one another because we can encourage each other in our faith. If you feel like you don't belong, look around — we need you!

Road trip

The LORD your God will go with you.
He will not leave you or forget you.

DEUTERONOMY 31:6

Has your family ever gone on a road trip, taking more than one car? If you have, you will know that it's hard to follow someone to a shared destination. What if only one car gets stopped at a red light, or the lead car simply drives too fast?

What's great about trusting in God's guidance is that nothing will cause Him to take off without us. He'll pull over if we get stopped and He will slow down so we don't lose sight of Him.

Following God may not always be easy, but we can trust that He'll stick around for the entire journey!

Doing good

People may be right in their own eyes, but the LORD examines their heart.

PROVERBS 21:2

Do you do the exact chores (and not one extra) that are asked of you with some complaining on the side?

What things do you do because they are the "right" things to do; and are you still doing the "right" thing when you are not happy about doing it?

Your heart matters! The condition of your heart and your attitude all add up to making a good deed good. So if your heart is not in the right place, you can do as many "good" deeds as you like and still not have done anything good.

You have to change your attitude.

God loves you

Nothing in all creation can separate us from God's love for us in Christ Jesus our Lord!

ROMANS 8:39

Have you ever played with putty? It can be stretched, twisted, shrunken or enlarged, but it is not easily broken!

Regardless of what tangled things we do to it, even if we break it into pieces, it will reattach, returning once again to its original state.

Our bond with God is similar, but all the more strong. Jesus' sacrifice on the cross immediately guaranteed an unimaginable love. Nothing can change how much God loves us. His love can bend to reach nearly impossible situations, but it will never break!

Shine for others

Do everything without grumbling or arguing. Then you will be the pure and innocent children of God. Try to shine as lights among the people of this world.

PHILIPPIANS 2:14-15

Have you ever traveled down a street at night that didn't have street lamps? The car's headlights light a bit of the path ahead, but we can still not see much. Street lamps are always helpful in guiding our way and keeping everyone safe.

What does it mean to be a "light" here on earth? Being kind to others, helping where you can, and living according to Jesus' example.

When we live like this, we will be like street lamps on an otherwise dark road, doing our part to light up the way.

The right focus

"Don't worry and say, 'What will we eat?'
or 'What will we drink?' or 'What will
we wear?' Seek first God's kingdom
and what God wants. Then all your
other needs will be met as well."

MATTHEW 6:31, 33

What does your closet look like? Is it filled to the brim with clothes? Are you one to stockpile your clothes, to ensure that you will never run out?

The more we think about things like the latest clothing trends, the more obsessive we can become and, soon, we are controlled by what we're wearing.

God knows our needs and will meet them. Imagine what we can do when we trust God to be our provider. What else could use your mind's focus? Let it go there!

Thinking out loud

People who are ruled by their desires think only of themselves. Everyone who is ruled by the Holy Spirit thinks about spiritual things.

ROMANS 8:5

Can you imagine what it would be like if we could read each other's minds? Does the mere thought of it scare you or make you feel shamed? What kind of person would others see if they could see your thoughts?

The things that fill our minds are the things we're investing in (if a relationship, movie, or popularity is always on our mind, that says something). We need to work on controlling our thoughts; doing so will keep us living godly lives that please God. What are your thoughts saying about you?

Copycats

Don't copy the behavior and
customs of this world, but let God
transform you into a new person
by changing the way you think.

ROMANS 12:2

Most of us are quick to copy others —
especially siblings. If we imitate our
sister who is misbehaving, we may be quick
to say: "Well, Mom, she did it first!" Mom,
frustrated, then so thoughtfully responds,
"Well, if she jumped off of a bridge, would
you?" No, of course we wouldn't! So why,
then, did we copy her misbehavior?

We have no shortage of people to follow in
our lives. But God is the only One we should
be copying in our thoughts and actions. The
more we try to copy Him, the more we will
grow to be like Him!

65

Keeping secrets

A gossip tells everything, but a true friend will keep a secret.

PROVERBS 11:13

It is such a disappointment when our favorite water bottle begins to leak. Initially, we might pick it up from the table and see a ring of water where it had been sitting. But we soon find that the leaking worsens.

Are you trustworthy when your friends share with you their secrets? Or, do you slowly start to leak things, telling one person, and then another? After a while, your friend will learn that you cannot be trusted; she may continue to spend time with you on some level, but will hesitate to share any secrets with you again.

Let's be true friends who know how to keep a secret!

God keeps you safe

The everlasting God is your place of safety, and His arms will hold you up forever.

DEUTERONOMY 33:27

Have you ever done a "trust fall," falling backwards into the arms of a friend, yet not knowing if they were going to catch you? As the name suggests, it is about trusting that your friend will, in fact, catch you. It can be a terrifying game.

When we face difficult situations, we begin to feel like we're falling backwards, not sure who is going to catch us (or if!). When we put our trust in God, however, we believe that He will catch us; and that His arms will remain. When it's hard to feel like anything is going right, our safety can be found in His presence.

Not alone

**The LORD will fight for you;
you need only to be still.**

EXODUS 14:14

Have you ever been told to "choose your battles?" If we were to react to everything that made us angry, even just a little, we'd spend most of our lives being angry!

When we're in a relationship with God, choosing our battles becomes all the more important — and much easier! There will of course be things that upset us and that we'll have to react to, but God can guide us in how to react.

Next time you're faced with a battle, take a deep breath and choose to let God handle it for you. The battle is no longer your own—God is in it with us!

God can do anything

Trust in the LORD with all your heart.

PROVERBS 3:5

Let's say, for a moment, that you are a very good gymnast. One day, another kid from school comes to you and says, "Sara can do the best cartwheels ever. Do you know how to do a cartwheel?"

"Um. Well. Yes, I can," you might say, while knowing that you can do much more than that! God looks at us and says, "You are not perfect, yet you can still do good things. So imagine what I can do, as a perfect God!" That's pretty hard to argue with.

We can usually do an okay job at caring for others, but a God who does not fail would do a perfect job. That makes trusting Him pretty hard to pass up!

God knows you

"Before I formed you in the womb
I knew you, before you were
born I set you apart."

JEREMIAH 1:5

A big party is coming up and you know the exact dress that will be perfect for it. Although you have not yet found the dress, you can picture it in your head. But, first, you need to either find it or make it!

That's kind of what happened when God created us. He could picture us before we were even born. He had big ideas about the things we could do and the places we could go. He knew the skills we would have and the ways He wanted us to use those skills.

Even before He laid eyes on us, He already knew us.

Being jealous

**If your heart is full of bitter jealousy
and selfishness, don't brag or lie
to cover up the truth.**

JAMES 3:14

I'm fine. I promise! I'm actually glad that you were appointed class captain and not me." Our jealousy can lead us to deny the truth about how we feel.

Nobody wants to come across as being jealous, but being dishonest is worse!

Hiding our true feelings only stops us from working through those feelings; and it keeps others from joining us in what we're going through (and, the truth is, we're probably not fooling anyone).

It may not be realistic to say that we will never feel jealousy, but what we can do is prepare ourselves for the moments when we do feel jealous.

Forgiving friends

Bear with each other, and forgive each other. If someone does wrong to you, forgive that person because the Lord forgave you.

COLOSSIANS 3:13

When you were first learning to ride a bike, your parents probably made you wear all sorts of protective gear. By doing that, your parents were saying: "We believe that you will ride just fine, but we also know that you'll fall sometimes; and, when you do, we want you to be as protected as possible."

Our friendships need protective gear, too. We are human. We will hurt each other whether we mean to or not.

We need to let forgiveness (our protective gear) have a place in our friendships — not only because others deserve a chance to be forgiven after they fall, but because you do, too!

Leap of faith

Love the LORD your God, walk in all
His ways, obey His commands, hold
firmly to Him, and serve Him with
all your heart and all your soul.

JOSHUA 22:5

Imagine climbing to the very top diving board, only to decide that you don't want to jump. Over and over, you climb up but back out at the last second, afraid of the risk that's involved.

It's hard to live for God when we're only somewhat committed to Him. We might think we're "all in," but when something scary, or out of our control happens, we may want to bail. If this is the case, we'll never really go anywhere.

Trust God completely and take that leap of faith.

Being an example

Always set a good example for others.

TITUS 2:7

Take a look at today's role models: movie stars, musicians, athletes and socialites. While we cannot judge the condition of their heart, the media portrays them in such a way that pulls us away from God.

The emphasis for most of them seems to be on fame, money and looks. But this doesn't really line up with what God wants.

We may not have as many followers as celebrities, but people are watching us. Those around us see the way we live and wonder if it is worth it to follow God.

Imagine the one or two (or several) lives that could be changed if you followed the example of Jesus in your life.

No more running

When I am afraid, I put my trust in You.

PSALM 56:3

When we're happy, we smile. When we're sad, we cry. When we're afraid, we ... what do we do? We might run, hide, scream, or fight. But let's consider a different reaction.

What if, when we're afraid, we trust in God? It may feel easier to run when fear hits us, and we can do that, but if we put our trust in God then we won't feel like we have to run quite as fast or as far (or maybe we won't even have to run at all).

Trusting God through the scary things can take away the fear that makes us want to run, hide, scream, or fight.

Make a list

**Each morning You listen to my
prayer, as I bring my requests
to You and wait for Your reply.**

PSALM 5:3

Do you remember how exciting it was to make a Christmas or birthday wish list? (Maybe you still make those lists — and it's still just as exciting!) It's exciting to think that we might actually get some or all of the things we're asking for.

Every day is an opportunity to make a wish list of what you need. While the people around us may grow tired of our lists, God will not; in fact, He wants us to bring our desires to Him!

Every moment with Him is a chance for us to speak our hopes and needs, and then wait and see what happens.

God chose you

**The LORD your God has chosen you
to be His own special treasure.**

DEUTERONOMY 7:6

What sweet memories do you have of times when you were chosen — chosen to play on a team, or to be someone's date? What about painful memories of experiences when you were not chosen? For many of us it could feel like we never get chosen for anything.

Not true, dear souls! We are chosen — and by the God of the universe, no less! Let's remind ourselves and others that we are chosen to be God's children.

While it is painful not to be chosen for a team, we can remember that we have been chosen for life by God!

God has a plan

We know that God is always at work for the good of everyone who loves Him. They are the ones God has chosen for His purpose.

ROMANS 8:28

You miss the bus to an important sports event, letting your entire team down. Later that day, however, there is an accident. Your spot on the team may have been risked, but your life was saved.

Sometimes, when things don't go according to plan, we assume that they have gone "wrong." Things will not always work out the way we want them to, but things will work out for our good.

God has already written the end of the story. We can trust Him with those details and look forward to the "good" to come!

God cares

**He heals the brokenhearted
and bandages their wounds.**

PSALM 147:3

If we get a deep cut, we need to keep it bandaged in order to stop the bleeding and protect it from getting infected. That bandage can bring us some measure of peace. With it on, we feel more protected — there is a layer between the outside world and the sore cut.

When our heart aches, God wants to serve as a bandage for us. He wants to come alongside us and be the presence protecting our hurting heart from the harshness of the outside world.

The healing process is not a quick one, but it is so much easier when we have God taking care of us.

Feeling good

Good people can look forward to a bright future.

PROVERBS 13:9

It feels good to do good. When we perform well at school, surprise a friend with a gift or help someone in need, we just feel good.

When, however, we're doing things we know are wrong, we feel guilty.

Whether we are aware of it or not, the shame builds inside of us. We are not full of light and joy, even if that is how we act. We have guilt and shame in us that will not go away by simply ignoring it.

Living a good life, on the other hand, is not only pleasing to God, it also fills us with light and joy.

Surprise!

> "If you give even a cup of cold water
> to one of the least of My followers,
> you will surely be rewarded."
>
> **MATTHEW 10:42**

When was the last time someone surprised you? A classmate offered to help you carry your books, or someone you don't much like paid you a compliment.

Small things can make a big difference, especially when done by the people we'd least expect. Who are the people who would least expect a good surprise from you? Maybe it's someone from your past who has hurt you, or the girl who sits alone at lunchtime because nobody thinks she's cool enough to be friends with.

Our acts of love do not need to be massive, but the little things can show great love.

Bursting with joy

I know the LORD is always with me.
I will not be shaken, for He is right
beside me. No wonder my heart is glad,
and I rejoice. My body rests in safety.

PSALM 16:8-9

It's wonderful to have days when we're in a particularly good mood for no good reason; no major event happened, it's not a holiday, a birthday, or a day filled with big and exciting plans.

The truth is, we always have a reason to feel as if we're bursting with joy! God's presence and protection in our lives should give us a lot to smile, yell and celebrate about!

There are (and generally always will be) a lot of sad things in our world, but we can share the joy of the Lord with others!

Loving others

Remember to welcome strangers, because some who have done this have welcomed angels without knowing it.

HEBREWS 13:2

How many times do you think you've walked past a celebrity on the street? Maybe you've even been in the same room as your favorite singer or actor without even realizing it! What would have changed about your behavior had you known that a celebrity was standing next to you?

There is nothing regular about anybody in our world. We are all wonderful, unique human beings and deserve to be noticed and cared for.

It is important to love everyone well, whether they are famous or not. That is what God wants from us, to love all His people equally.

God's family

You are no longer strangers.
You are citizens along with all
of God's holy people.
You are members of God's family.

EPHESIANS 2:19

What's it like in your home when one person is in a horrible mood? It sort of ruins the cheerful vibe of the house, doesn't it? Everyone knows that something is wrong and generally, we want to help.

The children of God belong to a great big family, and not all of us are going to always be okay. We need one another (sometimes you'll need me, other times I'll need you).

This family should pick us up when we're having a hard time — it is, indeed, one of the sweetest parts about belonging to a love-filled family.

Answers to prayer

When you ask, you do not receive
because the reason you ask is wrong.
You want things so you can use them
for your own pleasures.

JAMES 4:3

Think about some of the things you've asked for. Did you want a particular bag because everyone had it, or a new bike because you wanted to make your friends jealous?

When we pray to God, do we ever pause to wonder why we're asking for something? No matter what we ask, we should think about what it is in our heart that makes us want to see this prayer be answered.

God already knows our heart, but if we're not seeing an answer to our prayer, it might be that we wanted it for all the wrong reasons!

Total trust

**God is our refuge and strength,
an ever-present help in trouble.**

PSALM 46:1

Where do you draw the line when it comes to trusting God? Imagine the scariest thing you can think of. Maybe it's easy to trust Him with the "somewhat scary" stuff, but when we start getting into this "unthinkably scary" stuff, we back away a little bit.

We shouldn't only have to trust God occasionally. He is not a semi-powerful, semi-all-knowing, semi-holy God. He is all of those things, and no matter how much terror we face, He is able to show up and catch us, even if the ground is literally taken out from underneath our feet.

God is here too

> "Whenever two or three of you
> come together in My name,
> I am there with you."
>
> **MATTHEW 18:20**

What do you bring with you when you gather together with friends? Maybe you bring a bag of crisps, or you might have photos to share from the previous weekend. You probably bring a bit of your frustration, stress and feelings from the day. And, your other friends are bringing similar things, too. That's a room packed full of food, stories, and feelings!

What we might forget is that God is there, too. Where we get together, particularly in a room full of believers, He is there with us.

How does it change your actions knowing God is present? Acknowledge Him, welcome Him, thank Him!

Sorrow into joy

**You have turned my sorrow
into joyful dancing.**

PSALM 30:11

After a difficult breakup or a failed test, we are in desperate need of some cheering up. Few things, however, sound as if they'll do the trick. We certainly don't want to celebrate our losses, but what if the pain of our loss could be connected to the excitement of things to come?

Maybe the pain we're experiencing is leading to something good! We need people who can remind us that more is in store for us than we think now.

It's okay to be upset, but we should also look forward to what might be waiting for us in the future. God can lead us from sadness to goodness in His timing!

Love in every way

"I give you a new command:
Love each other. You must love
each other as I have loved you."

JOHN 13:34

How many different ways are there to love other people? That's a pretty difficult question to answer! There are probably as many ways as there are people! God tells us to love people.

We are not given specific instructions; all we need to do is love.

It might be in a normal way, like writing a love letter to our boyfriend, or it could be as simple as helping your mom clean the house.

No matter which way you choose, love is possible, and we are the ones who get to pour it out onto others!

God will never leave

> "Don't be afraid, because the
> LORD your God will be with
> you everywhere you go."

JOSHUA 1:9

It's a tough thing to swallow when our best friend moves away, our favorite teacher leaves the school, or our beloved family pet passes away. These things happen, but it still leaves us with questions and a broken heart.

God will not leave you. He not only created you, He dreamed you up. He is Immanuel, which means God with us — so He will not be without us! To do so would go against the very nature of who God is. He promises to never leave us and He will keep His promise.

It's not fair!

I will thank the LORD because He is just; I will sing praise to the name of the Lord Most High.

PSALM 7:17

Imagine getting in trouble for a wrong that both you and your best friend committed, except you are the only one who was punished! How unfair is that? If the roles were reversed, however, and we got off scot-free while our best friend was harshly punished, that really wouldn't feel very good either, would it?

If we're being honest, we all wish that life was fair. But life doesn't always work that way.

Our God is a God who is all about justice though. He gives everyone a chance, and no one can escape His punishment unless they ask for forgiveness.

You are special

You knit me together in my mother's womb. I praise You because I am fearfully and wonderfully made. My frame was not hidden from You.

PSALM 139:13-15

Can you believe that you are treasured enough to have been knit together by God uniquely and personally? We are not mass-produced — we are completely unique, each nose, toe and tiny hair is hand designed!

No one knows our details more deeply and fully than God. He not only knows them, but He chose them. You didn't accidentally slip past Him when you were being formed and, instead, received the craftsmanship of a rookie. You were hand-shaped by God!

A ray of sunshine

**This is the day that the LORD has made;
let us rejoice and be glad in it.**

PSALM 118:24

Have you ever seen a cartoon where a rain cloud follows around just one of the characters the entire time, while the rest of the world is sunny? Not only does that character look miserable, but nobody else wants to be around him, either.

It's not hard for our complaints to take over our lives and, before we know it, we're carrying around a rain cloud of our own.

Not all of life is sunshine, of course, but we have hope, so our complaints should not affect us as much.

Keep your eyes on God and you'll turn into a ray of sunshine.

Feeling sorry

**If we confess our sins to God,
He can always be trusted to forgive us
and take our sins away.**

1 JOHN 1:9

What happens when you get caught doing something you shouldn't be doing? Does your heart beat fast and your cheeks get hot? Do you want to run and hide, or immediately start trying to explain yourself?

We know that we will all sin. But what we do when we've sinned is what's important. When we do something wrong, do we feel sorry or nothing at all?

God wants to see our negative behavior lead us to changing our hearts. So when you sin, tell God how sorry you are and do your very best to never do it again.

How exciting!

What God has planned for people who love Him is more than eyes have seen or ears have heard. It has never even entered our minds!

1 CORINTHIANS 2:9

How fun is it when we finish opening all of our birthday presents and then a friend steps forward and says, "Nope! You're not done yet! I have a gift for you, too!" How exciting!

There is a lot in store for us in our life with God. We are still waiting to see what else God does through us and for us.

Isn't it exciting to know that God is not done yet? He is still playing an active role in our world and He has told us that there are wonderful things still to come. That's a lot to look forward to!

Mallory Larsen received her master's degree in Theology and Culture from The Seattle School of Theology and Psychology. She has an immovable belief that storytelling can better people, teach them and connect them. Mallory is the daughter of well-known Christian author, Carolyn Larsen. She is married to Darren and lives in Tacoma, Washington. They are proud parents of an adorable daughter. Visit Mallory at her website: www.malloryredmond.com